TABLE OF CONTENTS

Investments That Fit You

How to Develop a Strategy Based on Your Personality Type

MOODY PRESS
CHICAGO

© 1995 by
AUSTIN PRYOR

All Scripture quotations, unless indicated, are taken from the *Holy Bible: New International Version*. Copyright © 1973, 1978, 1984, International Bible Society. Used by permission of Zondervan Publishing House. All rights reserved.

ISBN 0-8024-3995-0

Library of Congress Cataloging in Publication Data

1 3 5 7 9 10 8 6 4 2

Printed in the United States of America

FOREWORD

I have known Austin Pryor for almost twenty years now, and I regard him as a good friend. As I have observed him over the years, I have found his counsel to be both biblical and practical. I know of no other individual with whom I would consult with more confidence on the subject of mutual fund investing than Austin.

I believe the true character of an investment adviser is not only the degree of success he has achieved, but the integrity that is maintained in the process. Austin has achieved success in the business world, but, more important, he has done so with truth and honesty.

Obviously you, the reader, must evaluate his advice yourself. No one individual has the right advice for everyone, and anyone can, and will, be wrong in the changing economy we live in. But if you will spend the time to read carefully the counsel Austin provides, you will find it both time and money well spent.

I encouraged my good friends at Moody Press to contact Austin about publishing his writing because I felt he had information that would benefit God's people. We are in no way competitors. Austin and I are collaborators in God's plan to help His people become better stewards of His resources.

Larry Burkett

The biblical principles reflected in this booklet are the foundation for the advice given in *Sound Mind Investing*, my book published by Moody Press. The material in this booklet has, for the most part, been excerpted from that book. As Christians, we acknowledge God as the owner of all. We serve as His stewards with management privileges and responsibilities. The practical application of biblical principles leads us to encourage a debt-free lifestyle and conservative approach to investing such as that shown in what we call the Four Levels of Investing:

Level One: Getting Debt-Free

"The rich rules over the poor, and the borrower becomes the lender's slave."
Proverbs 22:7

Paying off debts which are carrying 12%-18% per year interest charges is the best "investment" move you can make. So, get to work on paying off those credit cards, car loans, student loans, and other short-term debts. Accelerating the payments on your house mortgage, if any, should also be your goal—albeit a longer-term one. It should be your first priority to see the day when you're meeting all current living expenses, supporting the Lord's causes, and completely free of consumer debt.

Level Two: Saving for Future Needs

"There is precious treasure and oil in the dwelling of the wise, but a foolish man swallows it up." Proverbs 21:20

Even if you've not completely reached your Level One goal, it's still a good idea to set aside some money for emergencies or large purchases. A prudent rule of thumb is that your contingency fund should be equal to three to six months' living expenses. We suggest $10,000 as an amount suitable for most family situations.

Level Three: Investing in Stocks
*"Well done, good and faithful servant. You were faithful with a few things,
I will put you in charge of many things."* Matthew 25:21

Only money you have saved over and above the funds set aside in
Level Two should be considered for investing in the stock market.
In Levels One and Two, any monthly surplus was used in a manner
that *guaranteed* you would advance financially—there are no guar-
antees in the stock market. You should initiate a program of stock
mutual fund investing geared to your personal risk temperament
and the amount of dollars you have available to invest.

Level Four: Diversifying for Safety
*"Divide your portion to seven, or even to eight, for you do not know what
misfortune may occur on the earth."* Ecclesiastes 11:2

Once you accumulate $25,000 in your investment account, it's time
for further diversification. By adding investments to your holdings
that "march to different drummers," you can create a more efficient,
less volatile portfolio. The single most important diversification
decision is deciding how much to invest in stocks versus bonds.
That's why determining your personal investing temperament, and
following the guidelines given, can be so helpful.

Free Upon Request

Articles that guide you through the Four Levels—help on getting
debt-free, saving strategies, and updates on specific no-load mutual
fund recommendations that are geared to your personal risk toler-
ance—appear in my monthly newsletter, also called *Sound Mind
Investing*. In it, I offer a conservative investing strategy based on the
careful use of no-load mutual funds. For a free sample copy, simply
return the postage-paid card included at the back of this booklet.

A Just-the-Basics Strategy Built Around Four Model Portfolios

I. There are five key principles I believe should be incorporated into every investment strategy.

A. The foremost principle is to diversify in order to protect your capital against unexpected economic developments.

B. Other principles include having clear-cut, objective rules for your decision making, staying within your emotional comfort zone, acknowledging your current financial limitations, and being realistic concerning how high a rate of return you can reasonably expect.

II. The Just-the-Basics strategy incorporates all of these principles by using stock and bond "index" funds in combination.

A. Three Vanguard index funds exemplify the price action in the entire U.S. stock and bond markets.

1

B. By combining these three funds, you can tailor-make the risk and reward aspects of investing to your personal temperament.

III. **We look at the historical performance of four different ways to combine the three index funds.**

A. The lowest-risk portfolio is called the *Preserver* and calls for a mix of 80% bonds and just 20% stocks.

B. The average-risk portfolio, the *Researcher*, employs a mix of 60% bonds and 40% stocks.

C. The above-average risk portfolio, the *Explorer*, invests more in equities with a mix of 60% stocks and 40% bonds.

D. The highest-risk portfolio, which I call the *Daredevil*, divides the portfolio 80% in stocks and just 20% in bonds.

There's a common theme that runs through much of the correspondence I receive...

...from the readers of my monthly newsletter. After listing assorted investment holdings, the writer ends with a question something like this: "What changes should I make in order to have a good investment plan for retirement (or some other long-term goal)?"

I respect these people. They are making a conscientious effort to be responsible in their financial decision making, but they're finding it a bit of a challenge. The problem they're facing is that many of their current investments were acquired helter-skelter as opportunities arose. Investments were not made with an overall strategy in mind. What should these investors do with what they already have? And, given their particular goals, where do they go from here?

This booklet will deal specifically with those questions by exploring a "Just-the-Basics" strategy. It's a simple approach to investing that reflects five principles I believe every investment strategy should follow. Whether you're single or married, young or nearing retirement, managing a trust, investing for college, or buying your first house, this strategy is flexible enough to work well for you! Here are the five principles.

Principle #1: Success in investing comes not in hoping for the best, but in knowing how you will handle the worst.

Always remember: Nobody *really* knows what's going to happen next. Some things can be predicted; most things can't. The tide tables, for example, can be prepared far ahead of time because they are governed by physical laws. The investment world is a colossal engine fueled by human emotions. Millions of people make billions of decisions all reflecting their feelings of fear or security, hardship or prosperity. To attempt to make reliable forecasts in the face of this staggering complexity is foolhardy.

Therefore, since nobody really knows what is going to happen next year, next month, or even next week, your plan must allow for the fact that the investment markets will experience some unexpected rough sledding every now and then. That's where diversification comes in. The idea is to pick investments that "march to different drummers." This means your strategy involves owning a mix of investments that are affected by different economic events. For example, you might invest in both a bond fund and a gold fund. When inflation really heats up, bonds go down (due to rising interest rates) while at the same time gold goes up (because investors want a secure "store of value"). To the extent that the price changes in the two funds offset one another, you have added stability to your overall portfolio.

Surprisingly, it is possible to assemble some lower-risk investment combinations that give pretty much the same returns over time as higher-risk ones. When that happens, such a mix of investments is said to be more "efficient" because it accomplishes the same investment result while taking less risk. Just-the-Basics offers you four portfolios that combine stocks and bonds in various combinations in order to reduce volatility and risk while still achieving attractive long-term returns.

Principle #2: Your investing plan must have easy-to-understand rules that are clear-cut.

There must be no room for differing interpretations. You must be able to make your investing decisions quickly and with confidence. This means reducing your decision making to numerical guidelines as much as possible. A strategy that calls for a "significant investment" in small company stocks is not as helpful as one that calls for "30% of your portfolio" to be invested in small company stocks.

In so far as possible, your strategy should not only tell you *what* to invest in but also offer precise guidance in telling you *how much* to invest and *when* to buy and *when* to sell. As you'll soon see, with Just-the-Basics you'll always know exactly where you stand and what you need to do to stay on course.

Principle #3: Your investing plan must keep you within your emotional "comfort zone."

Your investing plan should prevent you from taking risks that rob you of your peace. Consider the four responses given in the Attitude Check. These are likely reactions from four investment temperaments or personalities that I call the Preserver, Researcher, Explorer, and Daredevil. In the next section I'll help you decide which one is best for you; for now, just recognize that *the amount of risk you take should be consistent with your temperament*. You shouldn't adopt a strategy that takes you past your good-night's sleep level! If you do, you will tend to bail out at the worst possible time. Just-the-Basics offers you four different portfolio choices, one for each of the four investing personalities.

Principle #4: Your investing plan must reflect your current financial limitations.

Your plan should effectively prevent you from taking risks you can't financially afford. The words "higher risk" mean that there's a greater likelihood that you can actually lose part or all of your money. Everyday, people who mistakenly thought "it will never happen to me" find just how wrong they were. Investing in the stock market is not a game where gains and losses are just the means of keeping score. For most of us, it represents years of work, hopes, and dreams. Its unexpected loss can be devastating.

That's why Just-the-Basics sets getting debt-free and building your emergency reserve as your two top priorities. Only then are you financially strong enough to bear the risk of loss that is an ever present reality in the stock market. I encourage you: Do not invest any discretionary funds in the stock and bond markets until your debt and savings goals are fully met.

Principle #5: Your investing plan must be realistic concerning how high a return you can expect.

I receive letters asking me to recommend safe investments that will guarantee returns of 12%, 14%, and more. If by "safe" it is meant that there's absolutely no chance of the value of the investment falling, then I must answer that I don't know of any investments like that. The ones that I do know about that are "safe" in that sense usually pay much less than 12%.

The reason any investment pays a high rate of return is because *it has to* in order to reward investors for accepting a higher level of risk. My goal is to help you get started in the right direction, incurring the least risk possible that will still get you to your destination safely. We'll look at the historical performance results of each of the four Just-the-Basics portfolios in order to let you know ahead of time what are reasonable expectations with respect to rates of return.

With these principles in mind, let's now take a look at the primary ingredients we'll be using to construct the four Just-the-Basics portfolios.

You know that a mutual fund is nothing more than a "basket" of stocks that a professional has selected from among thousands, and he hopes they will be good performers. But inevitably he misses some really excellent ones. If you could just buy *all* the stocks out there, you'd be sure to own *all* the good ones. Of course, you'd have lots of weak ones too, but if the economy grows, there will be many more strong ones than weak ones.

That's where "index" funds come in. I'll explain the index concept using the Vanguard funds starting with their Vanguard's Index Trust: Extended Market Portfolio. (Many fund organizations offer index funds, but the ones from Vanguard are especially well suited to this approach.) It attempts to provide investment results that correspond to the price and yield performance of 4,500 smaller-to-medium size U.S. companies. Naturally, it can't invest in all 4,500, but by using some fancy computer-driven statistical techniques, it buys about 1,400 stocks that, when taken together in the right proportions, act pretty much the same as if all 4,500 were present and accounted for. (It's sort of like when the news people take exit interviews at election time and tell us who the winners are going to be based on how a small number of people voted.)

Another Vanguard fund will also play an important role: the Index Trust: 500 Portfolio. This fund tries to do the same thing but with the larger-size S&P 500 stocks instead. Now, here's the neat thing about these two funds: *None of their holdings overlap!* This means that if you invest in both of them, you are essentially investing in 5,000 different stocks ranging from the very small to the very large. *The end result is that you've pretty much invested in the entire American stock market.*

Finally, we need to add the Vanguard Index: Total Bond Market Fund to our arsenal. This fund does in the world of bonds what the other two funds do in the world of stocks: acts as if it owns them all. It's designed to track the Lehman Brothers Aggregate Bond Index of more than 6,000 high-quality bonds of varying maturities. The Vanguard Bond Market Fund has an average bond quality rating of AAA and weighted maturity of around nine years.

We'll put together these three funds, all of them no-load, in different combinations...

...so as to produce four representative portfolios that are appropriate for the four investing temperaments mentioned earlier. We'll start with the Preserver portfolio. This one is designed to incur minimum risk in an attempt to preserve capital. Investing-by-lending (explained in greater detail in the *Bonds* booklet in this series) is the lowest risk kind of investing. Therefore, we want to have the overwhelming majority of the Preserver portfolio — 80% — invested in bonds. In that way, only 20% of the portfolio is exposed to stock market risk. We'll split the 20% stock allocation into two parts, putting half in dividend-paying large company stocks and half in higher-risk small company growth stocks. If we were applying the Preserver portfolio guidelines to a $40,000 Vanguard account, the holdings would be $32,000 in the Total

Bond Market fund, $4,000 in the Index 500 fund, and $4,000 in the Index Extended fund.

Now let's jump to the other end of the risk spectrum and put together a Daredevil portfolio. Here the goal is to make the capital grow as quickly as possible; dividend income is not a consideration. Obviously that means a major commitment—80%—to the stock market. Again, we'll split the stock allocation into two parts, putting half in high quality large company stocks and half in higher-risk small company growth stocks. The remaining 20% will go into Total Bond Market, not because we need the dividend income but in order to somewhat dampen *risk and volatility*. Here's what a portfolio would look like if we were applying the Daredevil allocation guidelines to a $40,000 Vanguard account: $16,000 in the Index 500 fund, $16,000 in the Index Extended fund, and $8,000 in the Total Bond Market fund.

As you would expect, the Researcher and Explorer portfolios fall in between these two extremes in setting their allocations. The Researcher is closer to the Preserver in risk, and uses a 40% stocks, 60% bonds mix. The Explorer is the next notch higher in risk with a 60% stocks, 40% bonds mix.

When you combine the three index funds in these various ways, you get some of the potential rewards of stock ownership along with a reduction in risk due to the less volatile bond portion. Sometimes the three funds will move together, but it will often be the case that the bond fund will move opposite the stock funds. When that happens, the price changes somewhat cancel each other out. The effect of this is to increase the price stability of the overall portfolio. Thus, although you are less likely to score a huge gain in any one year holding a combination of the three funds, you are also unlikely to incur a huge loss. This improved price stability (which equates to lower risk) is one of the primary advantages of diversifying through mutual funds for the average investor. For a look at how each of the four Just-the-Basics portfolios performed during the past decade, see pages 18-21.

A housekeeping chore investors must deal with from time to time is "re-balancing" their portfolios.

It's like four people playing a game of Monopoly. Everybody starts out with 25% of the money, but after a few rounds of play, some are richer and some poorer. To get back where you started, you'd have to "re-balance" by taking money from some players and giving it to others. Here's how that applies here. Assume you invest along the lines recommended for those with Researcher temperaments. You divide your money among the three Vanguard funds: 60% in Total Bond Market, 20% in Index 500, and 20% in Index Extended Market. In the months that follow, as some funds do better than others, the percentages you started with begin to change. If Index Extended Market does better than Index 500, for example, it may soon represent 25% of your total holdings while Index 500 falls to just 15%. How long do you let this continue before you step in and sell some Extended Market in order to return its value to just 20%

of your portfolio? How long, in other words, before you re-balance? I suggest the first week of each new year. Emotionally, January is a good time for new beginnings and fresh starts.

You will notice that re-balancing takes money away from your star performers and gives it to the poorer performing groups.

A common question is: "Wouldn't it be better to leave the existing funds alone and invest new money into the weak fund groups in order to achieve the suggested percentages?" If "better" means "more profitable," then the answer is that some years it would be better but I think most years it would not. Market performance leaders change as the economy goes through the various stages of its cycle. In 1990, the worst performance among the four major equity fund categories reported in *Barron's* was in the Aggressive Growth category (-9.9%). If you had not re-balanced and built that portion of your portfolio back up to its recommended percent allocation, you would have been underinvested in Aggressive Growth funds in 1991 when they turned in the best performance of any group (+47.8%). Or consider the contrast between quality bonds and high yield "junk" bonds. In 1990, junk bonds fell -11.5% while the high quality group gained 7.4%. If you didn't re-balance, you'd have been underinvested in the junk group in 1991 when it jumped 37.1% compared to 15.4% for the quality funds. I assure you, this kind of thing happens all the time. If it didn't, wouldn't the markets be a great place to make easy money? ◆

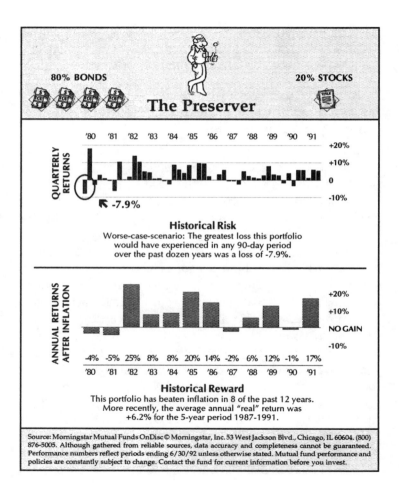

80% BONDS   **20% STOCKS**

The Preserver

'80 '81 '82 '83 '84 '85 '86 '87 '88 '89 '90 '91

QUARTERLY RETURNS

+20%
+10%
0
-10%

↖ -7.9%

Historical Risk
Worse-case-scenario: The greatest loss this portfolio
would have experienced in any 90-day period
over the past dozen years was a loss of -7.9%.

ANNUAL RETURNS AFTER INFLATION

+20%
+10%
NO GAIN
-10%

| -4% | -5% | 25% | 8% | 8% | 20% | 14% | -2% | 6% | 12% | -1% | 17% |
| '80 | '81 | '82 | '83 | '84 | '85 | '86 | '87 | '88 | '89 | '90 | '91 |

Historical Reward
This portfolio has beaten inflation in 8 of the past 12 years.
More recently, the average annual "real" return was
+6.2% for the 5-year period 1987-1991.

Source: Morningstar Mutual Funds OnDisc © Morningstar, Inc. 53 West Jackson Blvd., Chicago, IL 60604. (800)
876-5005. Although gathered from reliable sources, data accuracy and completeness cannot be guaranteed.
Performance numbers reflect periods ending 6/30/92 unless otherwise stated. Mutual fund performance and
policies are constantly subject to change. Contact the fund for current information before you invest.

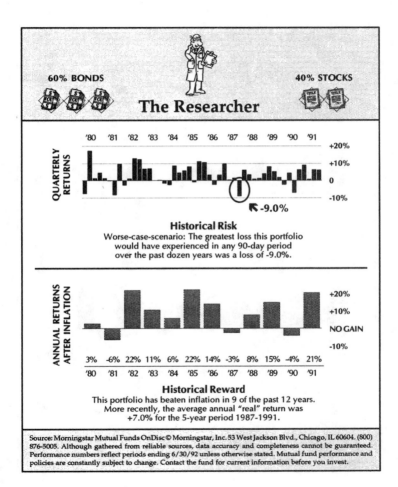

60% BONDS

The Researcher

40% STOCKS

Historical Risk
Worse-case-scenario: The greatest loss this portfolio
would have experienced in any 90-day period
over the past dozen years was a loss of -9.0%.

'80	'81	'82	'83	'84	'85	'86	'87	'88	'89	'90	'91
3%	-6%	22%	11%	6%	22%	14%	-3%	8%	15%	-4%	21%

Historical Reward
This portfolio has beaten inflation in 9 of the past 12 years.
More recently, the average annual "real" return was
+7.0% for the 5-year period 1987-1991.

Source: Morningstar Mutual Funds OnDisc © Morningstar, Inc. 53 West Jackson Blvd., Chicago, IL 60604. (800)
876-5005. Although gathered from reliable sources, data accuracy and completeness cannot be guaranteed.
Performance numbers reflect periods ending 6/30/92 unless otherwise stated. Mutual fund performance and
policies are constantly subject to change. Contact the fund for current information before you invest.

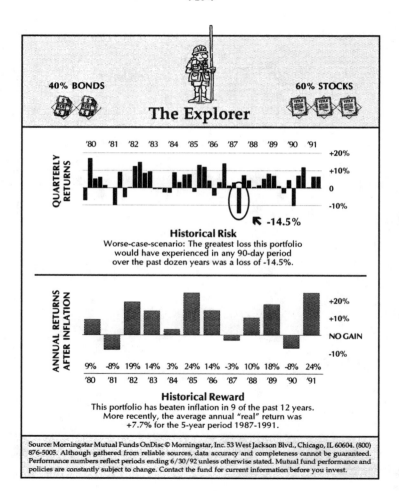

40% BONDS

The Explorer

60% STOCKS

QUARTERLY RETURNS

'80 '81 '82 '83 '84 '85 '86 '87 '88 '89 '90 '91

+20%
+10%
0
-10%

↖ -14.5%

Historical Risk
Worse-case-scenario: The greatest loss this portfolio
would have experienced in any 90-day period
over the past dozen years was a loss of -14.5%.

ANNUAL RETURNS AFTER INFLATION

+20%
+10%
NO GAIN
-10%

9%	-8%	19%	14%	3%	24%	14%	-3%	10%	18%	-8%	24%
'80	'81	'82	'83	'84	'85	'86	'87	'88	'89	'90	'91

Historical Reward
This portfolio has beaten inflation in 9 of the past 12 years.
More recently, the average annual "real" return was
+7.7% for the 5-year period 1987-1991.

Source: Morningstar Mutual Funds OnDisc © Morningstar, Inc. 53 West Jackson Blvd., Chicago, IL 60604. (800)
876-5005. Although gathered from reliable sources, data accuracy and completeness cannot be guaranteed.
Performance numbers reflect periods ending 6/30/92 unless otherwise stated. Mutual fund performance and
policies are constantly subject to change. Contact the fund for current information before you invest.

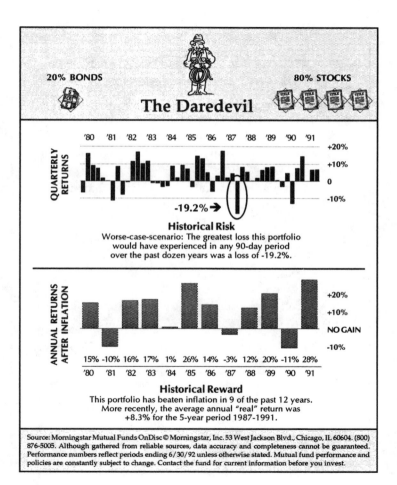

20% BONDS

80% STOCKS

The Daredevil

QUARTERLY RETURNS

'80 '81 '82 '83 '84 '85 '86 '87 '88 '89 '90 '91

+20%
+10%
0
-10%

-19.2% →

Historical Risk

Worse-case-scenario: The greatest loss this portfolio
would have experienced in any 90-day period
over the past dozen years was a loss of -19.2%.

ANNUAL RETURNS AFTER INFLATION

+20%
+10%
NO GAIN
-10%

15%	-10%	16%	17%	1%	26%	14%	-3%	12%	20%	-11%	28%
'80	'81	'82	'83	'84	'85	'86	'87	'88	'89	'90	'91

Historical Reward

This portfolio has beaten inflation in 9 of the past 12 years.
More recently, the average annual "real" return was
+8.3% for the 5-year period 1987-1991.

Source: Morningstar Mutual Funds OnDisc © Morningstar, Inc. 53 West Jackson Blvd., Chicago, IL 60604. (800)
876-5005. Although gathered from reliable sources, data accuracy and completeness cannot be guaranteed.
Performance numbers reflect periods ending 6/30/92 unless otherwise stated. Mutual fund performance and
policies are constantly subject to change. Contact the fund for current information before you invest.

Selecting the Portfolio Best Suited to Your Personal Temperament and Time Frame

2

I. Each of us has a "money personality" that reflects our attitudes toward earning, spending, saving, and investing money.

    A. Psychologist Kathleen Gurney has conducted nationwide surveys and found that people have a financial self and use money as a means to gain security, freedom, love, respect, power, and happiness.

    B. Gurney notes nine distinct money personality types, but I have combined several in developing the four investing temperaments in the Sound Mind Investing strategy.

II. Meet the Preserver, Researcher, Explorer, and Daredevil.

    A. Each of these investing personalities reflects a different emotional reaction to risk taking.

    B. A series of "attitudinal snapshots" should enable you to select the one that is closest to the way you feel about financial security and the trade-offs between risk and reward.

III. It's important to have realistic expectations with respect to investment performance.

A. Over many years, it is generally reasonable to expect returns in the 10% per year range.

B. This long-term result hides the often-frightening short-term volatility, which grows more severe as the proportion of stocks to the overall portfolio increases.

"Not only do we have a physical self, an emotional self, and a social self, but we have a financial, or money, self.

"This money self is an integral part of our behavioral repertoire and influences the way we interact with our money. In other words, your money personality is a major factor in how you utilize your money. Most of us fail to realize the extent to which our money personality impacts our financial habits and affects the degree of satisfaction we get from what money we have. There is an inseparable link between our unconscious feelings about money and the way in which we earn it, spend it, save it, and invest it."

This observation is made by Kathleen Gurney in her book *Your Money Personality*. She adds that psychologists believe that money is a kind of "emotional currency" that symbolizes many of our unconscious needs and desires, among them:

● **security**   (If I have enough money, I'll always be safe. No person and no catastrophe can harm me.)

● **freedom**   (If I have enough money, I can freely choose my jobs or choose not to work; my options are open.)

● **love**   (If I have enough money, more people will care about me. Money makes relationships a lot easier.)

● **respect**   (If I have enough money, everyone will recognize that I have merit, that I accomplished what I set out to do.)

- **power** (If I have enough money, nobody will ever push me around. I will be strong and have total control over my life.)

- **happiness** (If I have enough money, I would truly be happy. I can finally relax and enjoy life.)

Dr. Gurney suggests that as many as nine different investment personality types exist (which she discusses in detail). To simplify matters, I have combined them in order to consider just four. There's nothing "official" about these. I devised them simply to help make this process easier and perhaps a little more fun. We all probably have some elements of each of the four types within us, so don't think I'm saying that any one type will fit you perfectly. But you may find that you identify with one temperament more than the other three. If so, you can learn something about yourself from this exercise.

I call the most conservative investors "Preservers." They tend to worry about their investments...

... because the risk of losing their capital is very real to them. As a result, they are usually quite cautious, favoring

CDs, government bonds, and only the highest quality blue chip stocks. This approach helps them to preserve their wealth but may not provide enough growth to achieve reasonable performance goals.

Sometimes their desire to be cautious makes it difficult for them to make any investment decisions at all.

If they can find advisers in whom they have confidence, they are frequently willing to rely on them heavily to assist with investment decisions. Realizing that they are safety conscious and must accept lower returns as part of the trade-off for safety, they usually have realistic expectations with regard to how much they can reasonably hope to make.

If you're a Preserver, the basic philosphy underlying all of your investing decisions is to preserve capital. You would agree with Warren Buffett, a legendary investor of our time, when he said there were only two really important rules of investing. Rule #1 is "Don't lose any money," and Rule #2 is "*Never* forget Rule #1."

"Researchers" also tend toward caution, but their self-confidence enables them to overcome their concerns...

...if they believe they have done sufficient investigation. Simply reading in this booklet that a certain mutual fund is recommended may not be good enough for Researchers; they may want to know more about that mutual fund and why I recommend it. They are willing to immerse themselves in facts and figures in order to get a thorough understanding of the strengths and drawbacks of the investments they are considering.

They can easily postpone making commitments because they want more information. Up to a point, this caution serves

them well. If overdone, their ability to make decisions is para-
lyzed because they will never know for sure that they have
all the relevant information. Researchers appreciate the self-
discipline imposed by following an objective set of guidelines. In addition, they have the long-term mind-set and pa-
tience necessary to stay with their game plan for many years
in spite of occasional setbacks.

"Explorers" are fascinated by the money-making potential of investing...

...but if they lack confidence in choosing the best path, they
often take refuge in the safety of following the crowd. They
are attracted to the latest trendy investments that are
dominating the news. The "thrill of the hunt" is the fun
part for them.

Explorers can be impetuous and often hop aboard a
new investment without fully understanding just how
serious the risks might be. As a result, their holdings
are frequently a random assortment of moderate-to-
high risk "good deals" collected over the years. Such a
portfolio likely lacks balance and has no long-term focus.
Explorers would benefit from a systematic, controlled-risk
way of moving toward their long-term goals.

"Daredevils" have plenty of self-confidence. They enjoy the investment "fast lane"...

...and are often found playing the markets on a short-term basis. The new issues market, stock and index options, and commodity futures would be areas of interest due to the opportunities they offer to make a lot of money quickly.

They often resist advice to diversify into more prudent, less colorful investments. Yet, even Daredevils need a solid, conservative base to counter their occasional impulsiveness and higher-risk tendencies. If they're not careful, they'll reach their retirement years with little to show for a lifetime of wheeling and dealing.

Daredevils could really benefit from the Just-the-Basics approach where we emphasize putting first things first. The use of highly diversified mutual fund portfolios, while not as high-stakes as some of their other investments, would bring a much-needed balance to their overall investment picture. It would go a long way toward countering their natural inclinations to "go for it."

Now it's time to select the temperament that best reflects your particular situation. First...

...determine how much time you have before you'll need your investment funds. If you're saving for retirement, how many years until then? If for college, how long before college days arrive? The less time you have to invest your funds, the more conservative you must be because an unexpected set-

back "late in the game" may not leave sufficient time to re-
cover. The time available suggests this schedule:

Time Remaining	Acceptable Portfolios
Less than 2 years	Preserver
From 2 to 5 years	Preserver, Researcher
From 5 to 10 years	Preserver, Researcher, Explorer
More than 10 years	Any of the four is acceptable.

This timetable reflects *my* personal sense of risk. Other investment advisers might feel more comfortable with less re-
strictive guidelines. For example, they might feel that a Daredevil mix of 80% stocks and 20% bonds is acceptable up until
five years before the funds will be needed rather than 10 years
as I suggest. Another might say seven years. All of us are
being arbitrary to a degree. The point is that as the time to
begin drawing on the investments draws ever nearer, you
should move increasingly to a more conservative approach. If
you've got 10 or more years, you can afford to take more risk
if you want to—but do you want to? It's up to you.

Another very important reminder: after you select guidelines that you feel comfortable with, *stick with them!* There
will be many temptations from your broker, well-meaning
friends, the media, and your own desires for higher returns
that will encourage you to "make an exception" or abandon
your guidelines altogether. You do so at your own peril.

You're now ready to select the investment temperament that best describes your attitudes toward...

...monetary risk-taking and its possible rewards. On pages 32-35, you'll find each of the four listed along with its corresponding attitudes on risk and profit expressed in a variety of ways. Read each of them carefully and thoughtfully. You might want to pencil in checkmarks next to the statements that you identify with. Which of the four temperaments has the most checkmarks? (If you're married, you should ask your spouse to study them as well.)

It has been my experience that most people have little trouble seeing themselves in one of the four. The identification is usually almost instantaneous. However, if you narrow it down to two and have trouble deciding between them, my suggestion is to select the one on the left, the more conservative one (risk increases as you move from left to right). Err on the side of safety and prudence rather than risk-taking.

Once you identify your money personality, check it against the guidelines you set with respect to the time remaining. Do your time-frame guidelines permit you to accept that level of risk? For example, you might have the emotional temperament of an Explorer, but if you're going to need your money sometime in the next four to five years, that is more risk than you should probably take. For the sake of prudence, you should move down the risk ladder (for example, from Explorer to Researcher) and adopt a more conservative posture.

But it doesn't work the other way. If you have the temperament of a Researcher, you shouldn't move up to the more aggressive Explorer profile simply because the time frame would permit it. *You should stay within your emotional make-up.*

THE FOUR RISK PROFILES HAVE DISTINCT STYLES OF INVESTMENT DECISION-MAKING

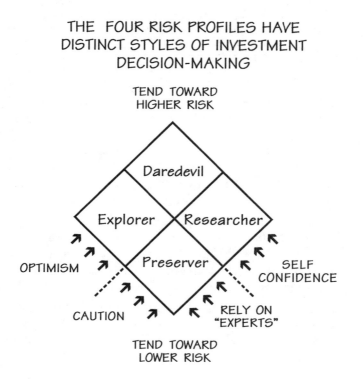

THE PRESERVER

❑ I'm very conservative, and am much more concerned about protecting what I already have than in taking risks to make it grow.

❑ It's important to my peace of mind to have stable, consistent year-to-year results.

❑ Making investing decisions all on my own makes me a little nervous. I tend to rely a lot on others to help me.

❑ The amount of current income I receive from an investment is important to me; if possible, I'd like to know the amount in advance.

❑ Preserving my capital and knowing how much current income I'll receive are much more important to me than beating inflation.

❑ News about such things as the savings and loan closings, our trade deficits, or the losses in "junk bonds" are a little scary and confusing.

❑ No amount of potential profit is worth risking the loss of 10% of my net worth.

❑ Making investment decisions is hard for me; I'm never quite sure I have all the facts. I wish I could be sure what the best investments are for me.

❑ It's irrelevant to me whether my portfolio does better than the stock market over the course of an economic cycle.

❑ If a stock doubled in price a year after I bought it, I'd sell all my shares.

THE RESEARCHER

❑ I'm fairly conservative, but am willing to take a greater-than-average amount of risk with part of my portfolio in order to boost its growth potential.

❑ I can handle the month-to-month ups and downs of investing, but I wouldn't want to end up losing any money for the entire year.

❑ I prefer to make my own investing decisions, but am always open to ideas from the "experts" which I search out in magazines, books, and television/ radio.

❑ It's fairly important that I receive current income from my investments, but I'm willing to accept some uncertainty as to the amount.

❑ Inflation is a genuine concern, but gains lower than the rate of inflation are acceptable if it means I can keep my risk down.

❑ I want to make my decisions based on a solid understanding of all the facts. I don't believe in investing in something just because everyone else is doing it.

❑ For me to risk 10% of my net worth in an investment that seemed to have a 90% chance of success, the potential profit would have to be at least four times as much as the amount I put at risk.

❑ Once I make a decision, I have a lot of confidence in it, which enables me to stay with it even if others around me are changing their minds.

❑ I keep an eye on what the overall stock market is doing during the year. Naturally, I'd like to do even better, but it's not a major factor in my thinking.

❑ If a stock doubled in price a year after I bought it, I'd sell half my shares and lock in part of my profits.

THE EXPLORER

❑ I'm willing to take a greater-than-average amount of risk in return for the possibility of having my portfolio grow substantially.

❑ I can accept an occasional year where I lose money on my investments, but I wouldn't like it if I had two of them back-to-back.

❑ I occasionally make my investing decisions all on my own, but usually I prefer to let my broker bring me what he thinks are his best ideas.

❑ It would be desirable to receive some current income from my investments, but I don't insist upon it in every case.

❑ Inflation is a genuine concern, so I'm willing to invest where there's a good chance of getting a "real" return even though there's a little more risk.

❑ I think exploring new financial territory is exciting. When I hear about the latest "hot" investment area, I like to take a look.

❑ For me to risk 10% of my net worth in an investment that seemed to have a 90% chance of success, the potential profit would have to be at least twice as much as the amount I put at risk.

❑ I don't have time to bury myself in the details like some people. I keep my ear to the ground and think I have pretty good intuitive insights.

❑ I do tend to compare the results in my portfolio with what the overall stock market did. It's a good feeling to know that you "beat" the market.

❑ If a stock doubled in price a year after I bought it, I'd hold on and hope for still more gains.

THE DAREDEVIL

☐ If I believe an investment has a chance of really paying off big, I'm willing to take the chance that I could lose a large part (maybe even all) of my money.

☐ I can accept losses in the value of my investments, even if they continue for several consecutive years. The end result is all that really matters!

☐ I almost always prefer to make my investing decisions on my own.

☐ The amount of current income I receive from an investment is not a factor in my decision making.

☐ Inflation is the number one threat. I think it's essential that you beat inflation, and that means you don't have the luxury of playing it safe all the time.

☐ I've had some super results on a few high-risk situations. Of course, I've had my share of big losers, too. To really make money, you've got to risk money.

☐ For me to risk 10% of my net worth in an investment that seemed to have a 90% chance of success, the potential profit would have to be at least equal to the amount I put at risk.

☐ I suppose I'm optimistic (and a tad impulsive at times), but I don't usually worry about my investment decisions once they're made.

☐ It's important to me, perhaps even a source of pride, that my portfolio does better than the stock market over the course of an economic cycle.

☐ If a stock doubled in price a year after I bought it, I'd buy some more shares in that company.

Being realistic in your expectations...

...is an important part of your investment planning process. Making assumptions (often known as "wild guesses") about the future is an unavoidable part of planning and budgeting. One fundamental question that needs answering is: "How much of a return can I reasonably expect from my investment portfolio?" It's important that your answer be grounded in reality and not wishful thinking.

To this end, I provided annual performance data for the four portfolios on pages 18-21. I could only go back to 1980 because that's as far as the index data went. But we all know the 1980s were an unusual time of economic growth and prosperity. The decade was hardly typical. In order to provide a more realistic guide as to what we might expect in future decades, it's necessary to include some recessionary periods as well. By substituting the Value Line Composite index in place of the Wilshire 4500, and using an older bond index to represent the Total Bond Index fund, I was able to carry the data back a full 20 years.

Bear in mind that the stock market's *average* historical returns from the past quarter century is about 12% per year, and the bond market's is about 8% a year. So what would you expect from portfolios made up of various combinations of stocks and bonds? Logically, you'd expect annual returns somewhere between 12% and 8%. And that's what I found: all four portfolios returned average gains of 10%-11% per year.

The accompanying graphic shows the surprising results: High-risk Daredevils wouldn't have done all that much better than the cautious Preservers over the *entire 20 year period*. There's only about a 1½% per year difference in average returns between the highest and lowest risk portfolios! The returns from stocks and bonds were sufficiently similar that the percent invested in each type turned out to not make a big difference over the long term. *Of course, for shorter periods the amount allocated to stocks can make a huge difference, as we saw in the Crash of '87!*

THEORETICAL
PERFORMANCE RESULTS
1972-1991

	Best Year	Worst Year	Average Year
Daredevil	33.7%	-22.6%	11.7%
Explorer	28.5%	-16.9%	11.4%
Researcher	26.0%	-11.2%	10.9%
Preserver	28.7%	-5.5%	10.3%

It appears reasonable to expect an overall return from your diversified Just-the-Basics portfolio, before taxes, in the 10% range. Bear in mind that these are "average" results. We know that if a penny is tossed 1,000 times, it's likely to land heads up about half the time. However, you can't count on these probabilities asserting themselves if you toss a penny *only twice*. It could easily come up tails twice in a row. In the same way, the longer you stay with your investing program, the more likely you are to get these kinds of returns. ◆

Moving Beyond the Basics: The Challenge of Fine-Tuning

I. Most stock funds have shown gains less than those of the S&P 500 Stock Index over the past 10-15 years, testimony to the inherent difficulties in attempting to "outperform" the market.

A. One way you can try to do better than the average mutual fund is by investing in index funds, as suggested in Just-the-Basics.

B. Another way is by continually fine-tuning your portfolio so as to stay with the stock funds that are doing best at the time.

II. The fine-tuning strategy involves both a process of elimination and a process of evaluation.

A. Along with other screening criteria the risk categories—as explained in the risk profile sections—are useful for eliminating all but 25-50 funds as candidates for purchase.

3

B. The process of evaluation involves rankings based on performance "momentum," which considers only the past 12 months.

At the start of the 1980s, the reigning media invest-ment superstar was Joe Granville. When he told his followers to sell everything...

...many of them stampeded to the exit door causing the Dow Jones Industrial Average to fall more than 3%—a loss equivalent to over 100 Dow points today—on the heaviest volume of trading in the 188-year history of the New York Stock Exchange up to that time. At the peak of his popular-ity, he once began an investment speech by walking across a swimming pool on a plank hidden just below the surface. Turning to the crowd, he exulted, "And now you know! I can walk on water!" But he failed to predict the start of the great 1980s bull market. As the rally began, he advised his followers to "go short" (selling shares with the expectation of buying them back later at lower prices) in expectation of profiting when the market collapsed. After missing the ma-jor market advance of the early 1980s, he finally turned bull-ish—right at the top of the market before the crash of 1987. By being one of the few analysts to recommend buying *after* the crash, his record over the past few years is once again one of the better ones.

Granville was replaced by Robert Prechter. He captured center stage with forecasts based on a rather mysterious theory of market movements and mass psychology called the Elliott Wave. He was the first to call for a Dow move to the then-incredible heights of 2700+, a forecast that was widely derided as absurdly optimistic. As that goal was approached, he raised his sights to the 3600+ area. There is some controversy as to whether he changed his mind in time to get his followers out before the 1987 crash. In any event, he has lost the great influence he once commanded and now spends his time writing articles and publishing books by other Elliott Wave scholars. He expects the 90s to be disastrous for the stock market and advises, "The 1990s will be the decade of cash. Stay in U.S. treasury bills."

And we shouldn't forget Henry Kaufman, then the chief economist for Salomon Brothers. He came to be known as "Dr. Doom" because his accurate forecasts of rising interest rates repeatedly sent shudders through the financial markets. His following gradually evaporated when he was too slow to recognize the sharp drop in interest rates that launched the bull market in bonds in the early 80s. Rarely quoted these days, he runs a money management firm that specializes in bonds. One respected Wall Streeter says: "Investors are always looking for a messiah. The system will always produce a new superstar, and inevitably, the star will fall flat on his or her face."

Market gurus come and go because it is impossible to predict future market movements with consistent accuracy. This is one of the reasons...

...that a majority of stock mutual funds have underperformed the general market averages. But the primary, and perhaps most puzzling, reason is that many funds are poorly managed. Although mutual fund managers are highly trained professionals, knowledge is not the same thing as wisdom. Sometimes they are simply mistaken about their stock selections. Other times they are guilty of poor market timing, selling heavily near a bottom or buying near a top (they are swayed by the emotions of fear and greed just like everyone else). The commission costs from excessive buying and selling, as well as the various operating expenses which run 1%-2% per year, also take their toll.

There are two ways to try to keep ahead of the average mutual fund. One is to invest in index funds as called for in Just-the-Basics. Then you'll know for sure that the results in your portfolio will be similar to that of the market as a whole. More often than not, this means you'll do better than the "average" fund. But if you're not willing to settle for that, your other option is to *continually* stand ready to adjust your holdings so as to own only those funds that are demonstrating relatively superior results *at that time*.

This fine-tuning process involves a lot more than merely selecting the leaders of the moment because...

...performance leadership among mutual funds is constantly rotating. The market is so volatile that this year's fund winners may very well be next year's losers. Numerous academic studies have shown that very few funds can consistently perform in the top ranks year after year. The evidence from these studies indicates that there is very little predictive value in using long-term past performance as a forecaster of future performance. *Consumer Reports* magazine points out that "few funds stay on top forever." Of the ten funds they rated highest in June 1987, only six remained highly-rated four years later. In fact, one of 1987's high-rated funds, the Fairmont Fund, dropped -12.6% from June 1987 through December 1989. The S&P 500 climbed over +15% during that time.

The best approach, it seems to me, is *not* to try selecting one super-great fund in order to hold on to it for many years. Investing in a particular fund, and staying with it for the long haul, is unlikely to result in outstanding performance over the entire period.

To be fair, I must admit that not everyone agrees with this assessment. *Forbes* magazine, for example, is well-known for its annual "honor roll" of funds that it recommends be bought and held through thick and thin. In its 1991 annual mutual fund issue, *Forbes* rightly points out that "this year's hot performer will be next year's laggard." But instead of acknowledging that some on-going routine maintenance is therefore necessary to keep your portfolio running smoothly, the magazine leads you on a search for all-weather performers that you can supposedly buy and forget about.

1986 FORBES HONOR ROLL

5-Year Performance AFTER making Honor Roll
9/30/86-9/30/91

Load Funds on Honor Roll	Sales Load	Annual Gain	$1,000 Invested
Fidelity Magellan Fund	3.00%	15.0%	$1,965
NEL Growth Fund	8.00%	14.4%	$1,800
Growth Fund of America	8.50%	14.3%	$1,785
Shearson Appreciation	5.00%	12.9%	$1,739
Amcap Fund	8.50%	12.5%	$1,650
Amer Cap Emerging Growth	8.50%	12.0%	$1,610
United Vanguard Fund	8.50%	11.4%	$1,572
Amer Cap Pace Fund	8.50%	10.7%	$1,522
MassCapital Development	7.25%	9.2%	$1,438
ProvidentMutual Growth	8.50%	7.6%	$1,320
Over Counter Securities	8.00%	4.8%	$1,160

No-Load Funds on Honor Roll	Annual Gain	$1,000 Invested
Janus Fund	17.2%	$2,210
Scudder Development	13.7%	$1,898
Nicholas Fund	12.2%	$1,781
Acorn Fund	12.1%	$1,770
Value Line Leveraged Growth	11.9%	$1,751
Twentieth Century Select	11.8%	$1,746
WPG Tudor Fund	11.2%	$1,700
Neuberger Berman Partners	10.0%	$1,612
Evergreen Fund	8.0%	$1,468

Avg Annual Gains of All 20 Funds	+11.6%	$1,675
Avg Annual Gains S&P 500 Index	+13.1%	$1,854
Avg of 11 Load Funds	+11.3%	$1,597
Avg of 9 No-Load Funds	+12.0%	$1,771

Forbes likes to emphasize a fund's performance in both up and down markets, with letter grades (from A+ to F) being assigned to indicate relative excellence. To make the honor roll, a fund had to roughly triple its shareholders' money over the past three market cycles (not quite ten years) plus earn at least a B or better in down markets. Sounds pretty good in theory.

Unfortunately, the results simply don't produce as advertised. In the graphic above, I've listed the *Forbes* honor roll funds from the September 1986 issue. You can see that the average performance of the 20 funds over the five years since these recommendations appeared was just +11.6% per year. This is *less than* the +13.1% gain turned in by the unmanaged S&P 500 index (which is often used to represent the market as a whole). Is this supposed to be outstanding and sophisticated fund selection?

Notice too that the honor roll recommendations obscure the advantages of no-load funds. The no-load group clearly outperformed the load group 12.0% to 11.3%, *and this doesn't even take the commission costs of the load into account*. When you consider the load, the difference is much more significant: The average no-load fund would have shown 5-year net profits of $771 for every $1,000 invested compared to just $597 for the average load fund. The honor roll funds were hardly outstanding.

Burton Berry, publisher of a helpful mutual fund ranking newsletter, which he calls *NoLoad Fund X*, performed an interesting study of mutual fund performance. He identified the 25 funds that had the best track records over a recent five-year period and posed this question: How many of these funds will be in the top performing group again next year? *The surprising answer was only one. He tried it again for a different five-year period, and the answer was none*! Altogether, he checked out 17 different five-year periods and found that, on average, only two of the top 25 performers of the past five years made the list again the following year.

These facts offer persuasive evidence that selecting mutual funds on the basis of their recent 5-year track records is not likely to identify the best funds for the coming year. Instead...

...we seek to initially invest in a top-performing fund that has been doing an excellent job of late. But, when the fund falters (as it inevitably will), we must stand ready to exchange it for one of the new leaders. How do you do this? In his newsletter, Berry proposes a way to measure fund performance that would pinpoint how to make the necessary changes. He devised a strategy which he calls "upgrading." His basic assumptions, which my experience bears out, are that (1) performance results that are more than one year old are no longer very meaningful, and (2) more recent months should be weighted more heavily than distant months. These assumptions led Berry to develop a methodology for evaluating mutual fund performance based on each fund's most recent one-month, three-month, six-month, and twelve-month performance. His approach also involves awarding extra rating points for funds that place in the top of their peer group for each of the time frames being measured.

Building on Berry's two assumptions, I have developed a ranking procedure which I compute monthly and use in the fine-tuning decisions I make when selecting no-load funds to recommend to my monthly readers. The major difference is that I assign funds to risk categories based on the nature of their portfolio holdings. Berry, for the most part, tries to work within the existing industry framework. Also, I have simplified the computations by omitting the one-month performance results and the star system for awarding extra rating points. I've made these changes in an attempt to improve the relevance of peer group rankings and to simplify the data gathering and computational chores.

As we begin to get into specific details, don't read through this as if it were a school lesson that you'll be called upon to work out on the blackboard. Instead try to understand the principles involved, and why they are consistent with what you have been learning. If you understand and approve of the rationale and decide you want to apply the strategy in your portfolio, you have three choices. One, you can subscribe to Burton Berry's monthly newsletter (see page 51) and follow his lead. I make no claim that my approach is superior to his, and I remain indebted to him for introducing me to the "upgrading" concept. Two, you can subscribe to my newsletter and let me do the work for you. Or three, you can do the research, data collection, and math calculations for yourself. You'll still need a source to provide you with the updated monthly performance data—which will likely cost you more than either of the above-mentioned newsletters. But it's a good way to build your understanding of the fund industry and increase your familiarity with the risks/rewards of owning the various kinds of funds.

Now, on with the show! Here is the fine-tuning technique for staying with the top-performing funds in each risk category that I have found quite helpful in making fund selections. First, you must go through a *process of elimination in order to reduce the huge number of available funds down to a manageable size.* This process is also referred to as "screening." In the Morningstar database, there are currently 2,371 load and no-load funds, and new ones are be-

2,371

1,087

913

774

528

339

131

47

27

NARROWING THE FIELD
OF STOCK FUNDS

We begin with 2,371 load and no-load
funds and narrow the list down to
only 27 finalists by using the
process described on the
next page.

ing added all the time. Let's say I'm looking for a U.S. stock fund which invests primarily in large, established companies, and seeks to buy them at bargin prices (i.e., it follows a "value" strategy). Here's how the screening process would work:

❶ Since I'm looking for an equity fund, my first step is to immediately dismiss the 1,284 fixed-income funds. That eliminates more than half the funds, leaving 1,087.

❷ Next I can eliminate any funds that don't invest primarily in the United States. That leaves 913.

❸ There are also 139 so-called "specialty" or "sector" funds to weed out. That gets us down to 774 remaining candidates.

❹ Also, assume I prefer to only use established funds that have been in existence at least three years and are at least $25 million in size. Eliminating the ones that fail these tests gets us down to 528.

❺ How many of these 528 funds have portfolios consisting primarily of large-company stocks? Only 339 of them.

❻ And how many of the 339 use a value strategy for making investment decisions? 131.

❼ Naturally, for my readers I'm only interested in recommending no-load funds, so I can cross off the 84 load funds.

❽ That gets me down to just 47. You can stop here if you like; the remaining criteria are optional. Because I have many readers who are just starting their stock market investing, I also choose to eliminate the funds that require an initial investment of $5,000 or more to open an account. Finally, since it's tough enough to outperform the market as it is, I sometimes take a look at the costs of running the fund (which are paid out of shareholders' profits). If a fund charges annual operating expenses greater than 1.5% *or* has a portfolio turnover rate greater than 100% (the higher the turnover rate, the more buying and selling and the more commissions being paid out), I might put it aside. If used in our example, these final three screening criteria would eliminate another 20 funds, leaving just 27 final contenders.

In less than 30 minutes, I've saved myself the time and trouble of seriously considering the other 2,344 mutual funds in the Morningstar database. Some may ask, "You mean, just like that?!" And my happy answer is "Yep, just like that!"

Now that we're down to a manageable few, it's time for the second stage—the process of evaluation. When assessing an investment's track record, the first question to be settled is...

..."which period of time are we evaluating?" Last month? Last year? The last full market cycle? *The answer to this question has more influence on the outcome of the ratings than any other single factor*. Most financial magazines use quite lengthy time frames when measuring performance and compiling their ratings. *Forbes, Business Week,* and *Consumer Reports* all use periods of five years and longer. I have found this to be much longer than is either necessary or beneficial. As previously explained, I typically look only at the past 12 months, giving greater weight to the more recent months.

Look at it this way. As the baseball season hits the mid-way mark, who do you think is more likely to win the league pennant this year—the team that has done the best over the past five years, the team that won last year, or the team that has been the most dominant this year and is currently leading the league? In sports, the teams that have been strongest of late are the more likely winners in the coming months. I evaluate mutual funds from the same perspective.

The first step in the computation is to ask yourself: if I had bought the fund *three* months ago, how much would I have made or lost by now? That gives the most recent three months' performance. Step 2 is to ask: if I had bought the fund *six* months ago, how much would I have made or lost by now? That gives the most recent six months' performance. Now notice something. The most recent three months'

No-Load Fund*X Newsletter

Provides all the data needed to implement the "upgrading" strategy explained in this chapter. Covers over 700 no-load funds and keeps you posted on current news in the mutual fund industry. User-friendly and consumer-oriented. Published monthly. Annual subscription $114. You can request information by writing to: DAL Investment Co, 235 Montgomery Street, San Francisco, CA 94104-2994.

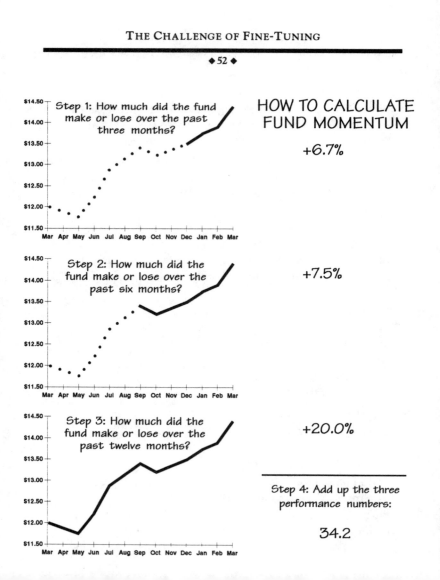

Step 1: How much did the fund make or lose over the past three months?

Step 2: How much did the fund make or lose over the past six months?

Step 3: How much did the fund make or lose over the past twelve months?

HOW TO CALCULATE FUND MOMENTUM

+6.7%

+7.5%

+20.0%

Step 4: Add up the three performance numbers:

34.2

performance is reflected in *both* answers. It represents 100% of the first answer and 50% of the second answer. This means that the more recent period is being given greater weight.

Step 3 involves asking the same question for the past 12-month period. Let's say the fund you're examining looks like the one at right. The fourth step is to simply add up the answers to the first 3 questions to arrive at what I call "performance momentum." Do you see how the momentum rating counts each fund's most recent three-month performance *three times more* than it does the twelfth month back? This formula thus incorporates both of the performance evaluation assumptions.

Now, let's look at the specific 27 large-company, value strategy finalists. On the next page, you'll find them listed in order of their momentum ratings. Seeing that the Babson Value Fund headed the list as of 6/30/92, that is the fund I would have recommended to my readers at that time. Out of the 2,371 funds we started with, this is the sole survivor. How long would I stay with this fund? Until a month came along when, after going through this performance evaluation process, I discover that the fund no longer ranks in the "top ten" according to momentum. When that happens (it usually takes between 6 and 18 months for a fund that was once ranked first to drop out of the top ten altogether), I would recommend selling the Babson Value Fund and replacing it with the fund that was ranked number one *at that time*.

In reviewing the data from the past six years, this strategy would have upgraded to a new fund about two times a year

ANALYSIS OF

FOR PERIOD

Fund Group	Name of Fund	Performance Momentum	3 Mo Return	6 Mo Return
Babson Fund Group	Value Fund	29.0	3.3%	9.3%
Price T. Rowe Funds	Equity-Income Fund	27.0	4.0%	7.6%
Bartlett Funds	Basic Value Fund	26.0	3.7%	5.7%
Scudder Funds	Growth/Income Fund	25.3	2.5%	2.5%
USAA Group	Mutual Income Stock	24.4	3.7%	2.2%
Vanguard Group	Windsor II	23.8	4.0%	4.1%
Vanguard Group	Equity-Income Fund	23.7	4.8%	3.6%
Neuberger Berman	Guardian Fund	23.6	0.5%	3.1%
Highmark Group	Income-Equity Fund	22.6	4.1%	3.5%
AARP Investments	Growth/Income Fund	22.6	2.1%	2.3%
SAFECO Mutual Funds	Income Fund	22.3	4.3%	4.4%
Salomon Brothers	Opportunity Fund	22.0	2.6%	3.8%
Price T. Rowe Funds	Growth/Income Fund	19.4	2.1%	3.5%
Copley Fund	Copley	19.4	4.1%	0.6%
Reich & Tang Group	Equity Fund	18.6	2.4%	3.5%
Harbor Funds	Value Fund	18.3	3.5%	3.5%
Lexington Group	Corporate Leaders	16.7	2.3%	1.6%
Dodge And Cox Group	Stock Fund	14.8	1.6%	2.8%
Galaxy Funds	Equity Value Retail	13.0	-0.3%	2.1%
USAA Group	Mutual Growth	12.1	-0.3%	-2.1%
Financial Funds	Equity Fund	12.0	-0.6%	-0.6%
Hummer Wayne Group	Wayne Hummer Growth	11.7	-0.7%	0.0%
Babson Fund Group	UMB Stock Fund	11.3	0.1%	0.3%
Vanguard Group	Quantitative Fund	10.6	0.3%	-2.2%
Primary Trend	Primary Trend	10.0	1.7%	1.1%
Babson Fund Group	Growth Fund	6.2	-0.0%	-1.9%
Vanguard Group	Morgan Growth	4.2	-1.9%	-3.0%

PERFORMANCE MOMENTUM

ENDING 6/30/92

12 Mo Return	3 Year Annualized	Assets Millions	Expenses Per $100	Portfolio Turnover	Minimum Purchase
16.5%	9.2%	$29	$1.01	30%	$1,000
15.5%	8.5%	1,494	1.05	33%	2,500
16.6%	7.2%	89	1.20	49%	5,000
20.2%	11.2%	759	0.97	44%	1,000
18.4%	12.6%	298	0.77	26%	1,000
15.7%	9.3%	4,080	0.45	20%	3,000
15.3%	7.7%	601	0.45	19%	3,000
20.0%	12.2%	710	0.84	59%	1,000
14.9%	6.8%	62	1.17	38%	1,000
18.1%	10.8%	547	0.93	41%	500
13.6%	6.8%	171	0.93	20%	1,000
15.6%	5.3%	99	1.30	10%	1,000
13.8%	7.8%	679	0.93	47%	2,500
14.7%	8.1%	32	1.38	7%	1,000
12.6%	7.1%	84	1.12	27%	5,000
11.2%	8.8%	48	0.80	22%	2,000
12.9%	9.8%	97	0.67	0%	1,000
10.4%	10.1%	296	0.64	5%	2,500
11.2%	8.2%	89	0.94	40%	2,500
14.4%	11.8%	380	1.09	36%	1,000
13.3%	11.2%	58	0.98	64%	250
12.4%	14.6%	56	1.23	3%	1,000
10.9%	9.4%	71	0.85	5%	1,000
12.5%	12.1%	348	0.43	61%	3,000
7.3%	5.4%	33	1.20	77%	2,500
8.1%	5.8%	242	0.86	22%	500
9.1%	10.8%	970	0.46	52%	3,000

on average (1988 was the highest with four, and 1986 the lowest with none). Berry contends that his similar approach resulted in gains exceeding 20% per year through the 1980s. Mark Hulbert, who publishes an investment newsletter that rates the performance of other newsletters, supports Berry's claim. Of course, that period contained the greatest bull market in history, so future years might not attain such lofty heights. But it is a proven strategy that provides strictly mechanical guidelines and is easy to implement.

Now you know how to use screening criteria as part of a process of elimination to narrow the list of investment candidates down to a few dozen. And, you know of a way to measure the performance of those surviving funds in order to identify those top few with the most persistent records of excellence over the past year. The final thing you need to know is how much of your holdings to invest in the various funds and risk categories. The table on pages 58-59 gives you my suggestions. Consider the allocations shown as being reasonable during "normal" market conditions. In my monthly newsletter, I make adjustments in these allocations from time to time. These adjustments are of two kinds. First, there are adjustments *between* the two major categories of stock and interest-earning funds. There are occasional periods when the stock and bond markets go to price extremes. These periods offer opportunities to buy or sell at unusually attractive levels, and the allocations can be changed to take advantage of that. For example, in June 1991 I told my readers that the price-to-dividend ratio of the stock market had moved to historically overvalued territory, and suggested a reduction of 20% in stock holdings across the board. This meant that Preservers who acted on my advice would, for a period of time, have no money in the stock market, Researchers only 20%, and so on. The money received from selling their stock fund shares could be parked in the money market for safety purposes.

Second, I occasionally recommend adjustments *within* the major categories. These involve swapping one kind of stock fund for another stock fund or one kind of bond fund for another bond fund. They usually do not have nearly the impact on your overall returns as the first kind of adjustment explained above. For example, in 1994 I increased the amount invested in international bond funds from zero to 10% in an attempt to protect against weakness in the U.S. dollar.

To simplify matters, don't be overly concerned with extreme precision as to the percentage allocations. If you have 12% in a fund when the table is calling for just 10%, it's OK. After a while, your original percentage allocations will change anyway due to market price fluctuations. *Plan to rebalance the overall portfolio in the first week of each new year* in order to get back in line with the original numbers. The important thing is that you have a plan and that you are broadly diversified. And remember, these guidelines are not absolutes—other market professionals might consider them too conservative or too risky. You should feel free to make minor adjustments as you think best for your situation. ♦

FINE-TUNING YOUR RISK

Your decision as to how much to invest in stocks versus interest-earning bond funds will have the greatest influence on your portfolio's performance. The percentages shown below are my suggestions as to how to divide your portfolio among the various risk categories for each of the four temperaments under "normal" conditions (see page 57). 100% represents the total value of your holdings, including any IRA, 401k, and other retirement-type accounts you might have but excluding your contingency fund and college investment accounts for the kids.

THE PRESERVER
20% STOCKS
80% INTEREST-EARNING

"I'm very conservative, and am much more concerned about protecting what I already have than in taking risks to make it grow."

International Stock Funds	None
Precious Metals Funds	None
Small Company / Growth Funds	None
Large Company / Growth Funds	10%
Small Company / Value Funds	None
Large Company / Value Funds	10%
Total Stock Portion	**20%**
International Bond Funds	None
High Yield "Junk" Bond Funds	None
Long-Term Bond Funds	20%
Medium/Short-Term Bond Funds	60%
Money Market Mutual Funds	None
Total Interest-Earning Portion	**80%**

	THE RESEARCHER 40% STOCKS 60% INTEREST-EARNING	THE EXPLORER 60% STOCKS 40% INTEREST-EARNING	THE DAREDEVIL 80% STOCKS 20% INTEREST-EARNING
	"I'm fairly conservative, but am willing to take a greater-than-average amount of risk with a part of my portfolio in order to boost its overall growth potential."	"I'm willing to take a greater-than-average amount of risk in my overall portfolio in return for the possibility of having it grow substantially."	"If I believe an investment has a chance of really paying off big, I'm willing to take the chance that I could lose a large part (maybe even all) of my money."
	10%	15%	15%
	None	None	5%
	None	5%	10%
	10%	15%	20%
	10%	10%	10%
	10%	15%	20%
	40%	**60%**	**80%**
	None	None	None
	None	10%	10%
	20%	10%	None
	40%	20%	10%
	None	None	None
	60%	**40%**	**20%**

Making the Transition: How to Get from Where You Are Now to Where You Want to Go

I. The "right" portfolio moves can't be evaluated simply in terms of maximizing profits.

A. No investment portfolio can be consistently positioned to maximize profits from coming events.

B. The "right" portfolio move looks ahead to your goal and has a high probability of reaching it (and may have to occasionally settle for lower gains along the way in order to protect capital).

II. The "right" investment portfolio takes into account the spiritual, intellectual, and emotional aspects of the investor.

A. The right portfolio moves are consistent with a specific, biblically sound, long-term strategy you've developed. They come after giving sufficient time to prayer and seeking Christian counsel.

4

B. The right portfolio moves should be reasonable, explainable, and prudent under the circumstances.

C. The right portfolio moves are consistent with your investing temperament.

III. A remodeling worksheet can provide an overview of how to go about making the transition.

A. The remodeling worksheet will list current equity and fixed-income holdings and allow you to conveniently calculate the percentage allocations between the two.

B. The worksheet will show you what changes in holdings are necessary to change your portfolio from its present structure to one that matches your investment temperament and long-term goals.

"Future shock is the disorientation that affects an individual when he is overwhelmed by change and even the prospect of change. It is the consequence of having to make too many decisions...

...about too many new and unfamiliar problems in too short a time...We are in collision with tomorrow. Future shock has arrived." —Alvin Toffler

Do you ever feel like that? As if the decisions you are required to make, especially about your finances, are coming at you at an ever faster and confusing rate? A great many people today are finding it increasingly difficult to know which is the "right" step to take. They wonder:

"Is this a good time to buy stocks?"

"Which money market mutual fund would be best?"

"Should I sell some of my employer's stock in order to diversify?"

"My CDs mature soon. Should I renew them for 30 days, 90 days, a year?"

"How much of my retirement plan at work should I put in stocks versus bonds?"

"If I sell this losing investment and buy something else, will I be better off?"

Since we cannot know the future with certainty, it's obvious that no investment portfolio that any of us come up with will ever be *perfectly* positioned to profit from upcoming events. As the future unfolds, it will always be possible to point to ways we could have made more money than we did — and some of them will appear incredibly obvious in retrospect! *This means that it's pointless to think of the "right" investment portfolio simply in terms of maximizing profits. If that is your approach, you will always be frustrated and second-guessing your decisions.*

The "right" portfolio is one that realistically faces where you are right now, looks years ahead to where you want to go, *and has a very high probability of getting you there on time.* As you consider "remodeling" your current holdings, let's look at some of the characteristics of the "right" steps to take.

❶ The right portfolio move is one that is consistent with a specific, biblically sound long-term strategy you've adopted.

One common trait that I find among many of those I counsel is that their current investment portfolio tends to be a random collection of "good deals" and assorted savings accounts. Each investment appears to have been made on its own merits without much thought of how it fit into the whole.

I find savings accounts (because the bank was offering a "good deal" on money market accounts), company stock (because buying it at a discount is a "good deal"), a savings bond for the kids' education (because they read an article that said they were a "good deal" for college), a universal life policy (because their insurance agent said it was a "good deal" for someone their age), a real-estate partnership (which their broker said was a "good deal" for people in their tax bracket) and 100 shares of XYZ stock (because their best friend let them in on this *really* "good deal").

In the area of investing, most people tend to be *responders*. They respond to sales calls, making decisions on a case-by-case basis. I want you to learn how to become an *initiator*—one who develops an individual investing strategy tailored to your personal temperament and goals. Then you can select the appropriate investments accordingly. The right investment step is the one that *you* seek out purposefully, knowing where it fits into the overall scheme of things.

> The plans of the diligent lead surely to advantage, but everyone who is hasty comes surely to poverty.
>
> PROVERBS 21:5

> The way of a fool is right in his own eyes, but a wise man is he who listens to counsel.
>
> PROVERBS 12:15

❷ The right portfolio move is one where you've taken plenty of time to pray as you consider trusted, experienced Christian counsel.

Because your decisions have long-term implications, you should take all the time you need to become informed. Don't be in a hurry; there's no deadline. A good friend once commented to me: "The Christian life isn't a destination; it's a way of travel." Likewise, you're not under pressure to predict the best possible portfolio for the next six months or make this year's big killing. You're remodeling in order to settle in for a comfortable investing lifestyle that will serve you well for decades.

Besides, prayer takes time. You need time to pray, ask for the counsel of others, and reflect. You should consider the alternatives, examine your motives, and continue praying until you have peace in the matter. If you're married, you should pray with your partner and talk it out until you reach mutual agreement. You're in this together and, rain or shine, you both must be willing to accept responsibility for the decision. The right investment step is the one that results from careful and prayerful consideration. This will add to your steadfastness during the occasional rough sledding along the way.

❸ The right portfolio move is one you understand.

This typically involves at least two things. First, it's relatively simple. It's not likely that your situation requires exotic or complicated strategies. In fact, the single investment decision of greatest importance is actually pretty easy to understand. Do you know what it is? It's deciding what percentage of your investments to put in areas where a return is uncertain (like stocks) as opposed to those areas where a return is certain (like savings). *This one decision has more influence on your investment results than any other.*

And second, you've educated yourself on the basics. When you're able to give a simple explanation of your strategy to a friend and answer a few questions, you've probably got at least a beginner's grasp. The right investment step is the one where you understand what you're doing, why you're doing it, and how you expect it to improve matters. That's the least you should expect of yourself before making decisions that can dramatically affect your life and the lives of those you love.

> The mind of the prudent acquires knowledge, and the ear of the wise seeks knowledge.
>
> PROVERBS 18:15

> The naive believes everything; but the prudent man considers his steps.
>
> PROVERBS 14:15

> Do not be anxious about anything, but in everything, by prayer and petition, with thanksgiving, present your requests to God. And the peace of God, which transcends all understanding, will guard your hearts and your minds in Christ Jesus.
>
> PHILIPPIANS 4:5-7

❹ The right portfolio move is one that is prudent under the circumstances. Does it pass the "common sense" test?

How much of your investing capital can you afford to lose and still have a realistic chance of meeting your financial goals? The investments that offer higher potential returns also carry correspondingly greater risks of loss. The right portfolio for you is not always the one with the most profit potential.

For example, it's usually best not to have a majority of your investments in a single asset or security. For that reason, people who have large holdings of stock in the company they work for often sell some of it in order to diversify. If the stock doubles after they sell it, does that mean they did the "wrong" thing? No, they did the right thing. After all, the stock could have fallen dramatically as well as risen. What would a large loss have done to their retirement planning? The right investment step is the one that protects you in the event of life's occasional worst-case scenarios. Generally, this moves you in the direction of increased diversification.

❺ The right portfolio move is one that is consistent with your investing "self"—will it fit comfortably?

I originally developed the structure of the four Sound Mind Investing temperaments to illustrate that, as part of our separate God-given identities, we each have different capacities to easily accept risk and uncertainty. Some people actually seem to be energized by the thrill of adventure while others prefer more secure, predictable surroundings. If you make investments that violate your natural temperament, you are much more likely to react emotionally when the occasional setbacks occur and objective decision making is needed.

When someone presents me with two investing alternatives and invites my opinion, I often ask, "Which one would you *like* to do, and why?" This is my way of learning more about that person's investing temperament. Unless I find a grievous flaw in people's financial logic, I encourage them to take the course of action they intuitively prefer. They are more likely to stick with their strategy over the long term and exercise the self-discipline needed to be successful if they are comfortable with their portfolio. The right investment step is the one that enhances your ability to make calm and well-reasoned decisions.

With these points in mind, it's time to walk through a "remodeling" project that changes an investment portfolio. I have designed it...

...to teach by example. Carefully follow the steps taken by Tom and Marilyn Randolph as they move toward the portfolio recommended for an Explorer temperament. I made these assumptions: Bank and credit union savings are federally insured; annuities are only as safe as the insurance companies that issue them; and 401(k) plans usually offer generic stock, bond, and money market options. As you begin, keep in mind these two guiding principles:

▶ You don't need to perfectly achieve the recommended percentages for the various risk categories. It's good enough to come close; when in doubt, go with less risk.

▶ You don't have to change things all at once. Take it

in steps over many months (or even a few years) as your comfort level grows.

Step 1: Make a list of the current values of your investable assets divided into two groups: investments where you are an owner and investments where you are a lender.

Basically, this means to write down the investments over which you exercise control. There are two exceptions. Do not include the savings set aside for your contingency fund. They are not part of your long-term risk-taking strategy. Also, do not include investments set aside for the children's education—these assets should go through their own remodeling process once you understand how to do it. If you are married, put down both spouses' investments. Married partners are in this together. I discourage attempts to keep "his" money separate from "her" money.

As you can see from Tom and Marilyn's list (page 70), at this stage you don't need to distinguish between his and hers, retirement or current savings, or when you bought them or what you paid. *Look past* whether the investment is held in a normal brokerage account, an IRA, a 401(k), a variable annuity or any other legal structure in which investments are placed. The goal is to list on paper your various investments and the amount you would expect to receive if you sold or exchanged them.

INVESTMENT HOLDINGS OF TOM AND MARILYN RANDOLPH

INVESTMENTS WHERE WE ARE OWNERS

$8,300	Tom's 401(k) at work invested in the "S&P 500" portfolio
$4,600	General Electric shares in Tom's ESOP at work
$6,000	Pension plan investment in an aggressive growth fund
$2,300	Goodyear shares inherited from Marilyn's mother
$1,900	Delta Airlines shares inherited from Marilyn's mother
$23,100	Equity portion is 35% of total holdings

INVESTMENTS WHERE WE ARE LENDERS

$8,300	Tom's 401(k) at work invested in long-term gov't bonds
$8,300	Tom's 401(k) at work that's invested in the money market
$2,600	Credit union passbook joint savings account
$12,400	Tom's IRA invested in a bank money market account
$2,600	Marilyn's IRA invested in a bank money market account
$3,000	Teasury bill inherited from Marilyn's mother
$6,000	Marilyn's pension plan invested in long-term corp bonds
$43,200	Fixed Income portion is 65% of total holdings
$66,300	Total Investment Holdings

Step 2: Record each of the holdings in the appropriate risk category in the Remodeling Worksheet.

This step helps in determining the amount of risk you are presently carrying. I have listed a few of the most common types of investments found in portfolios. They appear as headings in the Remodeling Worksheet (next page). Risk generally decreases as you move from left to right across the worksheet. (The placement of the various investment categories reflects my personal opinion—there is no "official" reference which ranks risk, probably because even within categories risk can vary widely. Quite often, risk is in the eye of the beholder.)

When you're finished, add up the totals and calculate what percentage each group represents in your total holdings. This is your first insight into how much risk you're taking in your portfolio (see pages 58-59 to review the suggested allocation guidelines for each of the four Sound Mind portfolios). Since the Randolphs' goal is to begin moving toward the degree of risk present in an Explorer portfolio, I have also provided a section for them to record the allocation percentages called for. Below the "desired" percentages, there is room to think through a few alternative ways they could change their present holdings to arrive at the desired percentages.

There is no right or wrong way to make the transition—it is mostly a function of your personal desires in the areas of: (1) how fast you want to make the transition, (2) how much flexibility (or how many choices) you have in your existing retirement accounts, (3) and just how precise you want to be. In the Randolphs' case, I have provided three alternative approaches: Alternative "A" is an attempt to highly conform to the Explorer guidelines; alternative "B" allows more flexibility and the use of holdings in nearby risk classes to fulfill some of the targets; and alternative "C" is a minimalist, slow-as-you-go approach. The route they choose is up to the Randolphs. It should be the one they find most comfortable.

The Randolphs' Remodeling Worksheet for Equity Portion of Explorer Portfolio	Real Estate Partnerships	International Stock Funds	Gold/Silver Coins/Bars	Precious Metals Funds
Tom's 401(k) invested in the "S&P 500"				
General Electric shares in ESOP				
Pension invested in aggressive growth fund				
Goodyear shares				
Delta Airlines shares				
Total for Each Category	none			
Current Percentage of Portfolio = 35%	0%			
Desired Percentage for Explorer = 60%	15%			
Alternative A — Changes Needed:	+15%			
Alternative B — Changes Needed:	+15%			
Alternative C — Changes Needed:	+15%			

It's at this stage that investors often "freeze up." Many people seem to find investing...

...to be a nerve-racking (if not downright scary) experience. Making investment decisions, and then watching the results unfold, can be stressful. Do you become anxious when circumstances compel you to make important investing decisions? Most of us do to one degree or another. If my mail is any indication, a great degree of financial fretting is common. There are three recurring comments that lead the list of

Sm Company Stocks	Sm Company Growth Funds	Lg Company Stocks	Lg Company Growth Funds	S&P 500 Index Fund	Small Company Value Funds	Lg Company Value Funds
					$8,300	
		$4,600				
	$6,000					
		2,300				
		1,900				
	$6,000	$8,800	none	$8,300		
	9%	13%	0%	13%		
5%	none	15%			10%	15%
-4%	-13%	+15%		-13%	+10%	+15%
-4%	-11%	none		none	+10%	+15%
none	none	none		none	+10%	none

ways my readers express their concerns:

▶ "There's so much at stake. I'm afraid I'll make the wrong decision."

▶ "I'm not sure I know what I'm doing. I'm afraid I'll make the wrong decision."

▶ "My savings aren't making enough now, but if I make a change I'm afraid I'll make the wrong decision."

What is the "wrong" decision, anyway? If you feel a wrong

The Randolphs' Remodeling Worksheet for Fixed Income Portion of Explorer Portfolio	International Bond Funds	Zero Coupon Bond Funds	High Yield Junk Bonds	Long-Term Tax-Frees
Tom's 401k invested in long-term govt bonds				
Tom's 401k invested in a money market fund				
Credit union passbook joint savings account				
Tom's IRA invested in bank money market acct				
Marilyn's IRA invested in bank money market acct				
Treasury bills inherited from Marilyn's mother				
Marilyn's pension invested in long-term corp bonds				
Total for Each Category			none	
Current Percentage of Portfolio =65%			0%	
Desired Percentage for Explorer = 40%			10%	
Alternative A — Changes Needed:			+10%	
Alternative B — Changes Needed:			+10%	
Alternative C — Changes Needed:			none	

decision is like saying 2+2=5, then you're off track; such thinking implies investing decisions can be made with mathemati-
cal certainty. They can't. This doesn't mean the economy and
investment markets are completely random, only that you're
dealing with *probabilities*, not certainties and predictable
events. Scientists can predict with great accuracy when the
next eclipse of the sun will occur decades into the future, yet
they can't tell you if the sun will be eclipsed by clouds and
ruin next week's picnic.

Long-Term Bond Funds	Fixed Annuities	Govt Mortgage Bond Funds	Short/Medium Bond Funds	Bank CDs & Savings	Money Market Mutual Funds	U.S. Treasury Bills
$8,300						
					$8,300	
			$2,600			
			$12,400			
			$2,600			
						$3,000
$6,000						
$14,300		none	$17,600		$8,300	$3,000
22%		0%	26%		13%	4%
10%		20%				
-12%		+20%	-26%		-13%	-4%
-9%		+10%	-26%		-6%	-4%
none		+10%	-26%		-9%	none

All of this is actually good news. It means anybody can play. It's like learning to drive a car. After a couple of lessons, you know enough to travel around town if you follow a few basic safety guidelines. After all, you're not trying to qualify for the Indy 500—you just want to reach your destination. In the same way, once you understand the concepts in this book, you're fairly well equipped for making whatever decisions you face.

Pretend you're in a contest where...

...you are to travel from coast to coast before the current interstate system was built. You can choose any route (but they're almost all two-lane roads), travel any speed, and take as much time as you want. There are no extra bonus points for getting there first—the only goal is to arrive safely. Everybody who does that "wins." As you drive along, you constantly must make decisions. Should you take the route to the left or to the right? Is there construction or traffic up ahead? Will there be a motel with a vacancy? There are no scientific answers to these questions. Every decision requires some powers of observation, the ability to learn from your experiences, and a little common sense. You rarely come to a point where the decision is obvious. It would always be helpful to have "just a little more" information—but the challenge of the trip is the necessity of making choices *without having all the information. Nobody ever has all the relevant information.*

Investing is a lot like such a contest. You can't know for

certain what lies ahead; anyone who would have you believe otherwise is lying to you. It's *because* we can't know the future that we diversify and stay flexible. This brings us to one of the few rules that investing has: Protect your capital! That's the only prerequisite for "arriving safely." When in doubt, take the safe route.

What the 1990s will produce in the way of dramatic change in the financial markets...

...is anyone's guess. The 1970s gave us listed stock options and the birth of money market funds. The 1980s produced a veritable explosion in the fixed-income investments and mutual fund industries. But in terms of the potential risks and rewards for the average investor, the advantages offered by either of the Sound Mind strategies—whether Just-the-Basics (Sections 1 and 2 of this booklet) or your own "fine-tuned" portfolio using the upgrading concept (Section 3)—include sufficient diversification for safety and a risk level designed to fit your individual situation. The importance of these attributes hasn't changed. Assemble a portfolio tailored to your individual financial personality and long-term goals, and peace-of-mind investing can become a reality for you. ♦

Nothing is more surely condemned to failure than a high-risk strategy pursued by a low-risk man; he will always flinch at the point before the strategy has succeeded, and will throw away his potential gains in an attempt to leap back to the security he actually prefers... To be a successful investor you have to be right, but in your own way. It is not only a matter of knowing yourself. It is even more important to be yourself.

BLOOD IN THE STREETS
BY JAMES DALE
DAVIDSON WITH
SIR WILLIAM REES-MOGG

Sound Mind Investing

THE FINANCIAL JOURNAL FOR TODAY'S CHRISTIAN FAMILY

Dear Valued Reader:

I hope this booklet has been helpful to you. If so, I believe you'd enjoy reading through a complimentary issue of my monthly *Sound Mind Investing* financial newsletter. It's based on biblically-based values and priorities (see pages 4-5), and gives you:

Help in setting and achieving realistic, personalized goals. You'll find no claims that I can predict coming economic events or market turns. Mine is a slow-but-sure, conservative strategy that emphasizes controlling your risk according to your age, goals, and personal investing temperament.

Very specific, timely advice. I recommend specific no-load mutual funds. For each of four different risk categories, I not only tell you *what to buy* and *how much to buy*, but just as importantly, *when to sell and buy something else*!

Monthly "economic earthquake" updates. I include an economic primer that will help you understand the implications of the unfolding economic tremors. Plus, there are data and graphs of various economic indicators that will be especially helpful in giving us fair warning if a crisis seems to be approaching.

I'd like you to have the opportunity to see these benefits for yourself. Send in the attached postage-paid card for your free issue—there's absolutely no obligation to subscribe. I hope to hear from you soon!

Free!
A Sample Issue of
Sound Mind Investing

PLEASE DETACH BEFORE MAILING

☐ Yes, send my free issue!

Austin: I'm taking you up on your offer of a complimentary sample of your monthly *Sound Mind Investing* newsletter. Please send my free issue and subscription information to me at the address below.

Name: _____

Address: _____

City: _____

State: _____ Zip: _____

Free!
A Sample Issue of
Sound Mind Investing